Tom gets his red bus from the box.

Tom gets his truck from
the box.

Tom puts his bus and
his truck on the path.

Press. Press. The bus
and the truck set off.

The bus and the truck
go fast.

Bella's doll is on the
path. Bump! Bang!

Bella is mad with Tom.

The bus and the truck

go back in the box.